BBQ RUBS

SAUCES

AND MORE

ROGER MURPHY

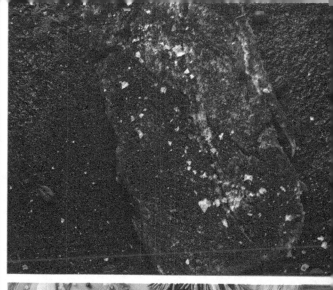

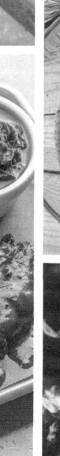
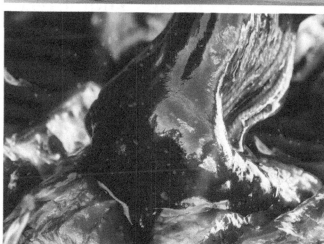

CONTENTS

INTRODUCTION

"ULTIMATE SAUCES COOKBOOK: THE ART OF MAKING BARBECUE SAUCES, DRY AND WET RUBS, SEASONINGS, GLAZES, MARINADES, AND MUCH MORE." WILL TURN YOUR BARBECUE ADVENTURE INTO AN UNFORGETTABLE CULINARY EXPERIENCE. FROM TANGY AND SWEET TO SMOKY AND SPICY, THERE IS SOMETHING FOR EVERYONE (WITH CLEAR STEP-BY-STEP INSTRUCTIONS) AND EXPERT TIPS TO ENSURE YOUR SUCCESS IN THE BBQ SAUCE WORLD. A GOOD SAUCE CAN CREATE A COMPLEX CARAMELIZATION AND FLAVOR, WHILE A WRONG SAUCE CAN RUIN YOUR BBQ MEALS. YOU'LL FIND MANY WAYS TO MAKE UNIQUE FINGER-LICKING SAUCE IN THIS ULTIMATE SAUCE COOKBOOK. THERE'S A SAUCE FOR EVERYTHING, WHETHER YOU WANT TO GLAZE YOUR GRILLED CHICKEN OR ADD FLAVOR TO YOUR ROASTED VEGETABLES. SERVE AN EXCELLENT BBQ WITH IRRESISTIBLE SAUCES AT YOUR NEXT COOKOUT WITH A COMPREHENSIVE GUIDE TO ALL YOUR FAVORITE FLAVOR

VOLUME (LIQUID)

US CUSTOMARY	METRIC (APPROXIMATE)
1/8 TEASPOON	.7 ML
1/4 TEASPOON	1.3 ML
1/2 TEASPOON	2.6 ML
3/4 TEASPOON	3.6 ML
1 TEASPOON	5 ML
1 TABLESPOON	15 ML
2 TABLESPOON OR 1 FLUID OUNCE	30 ML
1/4 CUP OR 2 FLUID OUNCES	60 ML
1/3 CUP	80 ML
1/2 CUP	120 ML
2/3 CUP	160 ML
3/4 CUP	180 ML
1 CUP OR 8 FLUID OUNCES	240 ML
2 CUPS OR 1 PINT	480 ML
4 CUPS OR 1 QUART	950 ML
8 CUPS OR 1/2 GALLON	2 LITERS
1 GALLON	4 LITERS

APPLE BARBECUE SAUCE

CHAPTER 1

SAUCES

APPLE BARBECUE SAUCE

THE INGREDIENTS

- Reduced-sodium ketchup – 1 cup
- Apple juice or cider – ½ cup
- Apple, peeled and grated - ⅓ cup
- Onion, peeled and grated - ⅓ cup
- Rice vinegar - ⅔ cup
- Worcestershire sauce – ¼ cup
- Yellow mustard – 1 tablespoon
- Runny honey – 3 tablespoons
- Chipotle chili in adobo sauce, minced – 1 tablespoons
- Freshly squeezed lemon juice – 1 tablespoon
- Onion powder – 1 tablespoon
- Garlic powder – 1 tablespoon
- Freshly ground black pepper – ½ tablespoon

METHOD

1. In a heavy pot, combine all the ingredients (ketchup, apple juice, apple, onion, rice vinegar, Worcestershire sauce, yellow mustard, honey, chipotle chili, lemon juice, onion powder, garlic powder, and black pepper).
2. Heat the sauce while frequently stirring until reduced and thickened.
3. Serve with barbecued meat of choice.

LEMON BUTTER SAUCE

SWEET ORANGE BBQ SAUCE

TOTAL TIME 20 MINUTES

THE INGREDIENTS

- Tomato ketchup – 3½ cups
- Orange juice – ¾ cup
- Molasses – 1 cup
- Wholegrain mustard – 1 tablespoon
- Garlic, peeled and chopped – 1 tablespoon
- Yellow onion, peeled and chopped – ½ cup
- Light brown sugar, firmly packed – ¼ cup
- Hot sauce – 1 teaspoon
- Worcestershire sauce – 1 teaspoon
- Salt – ½ teaspoon
- Cayenne – ¼ teaspoon
- Fresh ginger, peeled and grated – 1 tablespoon
- Freshly ground black pepper – ¼ teaspoon

METHOD

1. In a food blender or food processor, process all the ingredients (ketchup, orange juice, molasses, mustard, garlic, onion, brown sugar, hot sauce, Worcestershire sauce, salt, cayenne, ginger, and black pepper, for 15 seconds, until smooth. You will need to scrape down the sides of the bowl and pulse 2-3 times more.
2. Store in the fridge in a suitable container for up to 14 days.
3. Use as needed.

LEMON BUTTER SAUCE

THE INGREDIENTS

- Unsalted butter, chopped into pieces – ¼ cup
- 1 garlic clove, peeled and grated
- Sea salt – ¼ teaspoon
- Freshly squeezed lemon juice – 2 tablespoons
- Freshly ground black pepper, to season
- Fresh parsley, chopped, to garnish
- A pinch of red pepper flakes, to serve, optional

INGREDIENTS FOR ⅓ CUP

METHOD

1. Over low heat, and in a small pan, melt the butter.
2. Add the garlic and salt to the pan and cook for 60 seconds.
3. Take the pan off the heat, and add the fresh lemon juice. Season with pepper and sprinkle over the chopped parsley and red pepper flakes.
4. Serve the sauce with fish, over pasta or rice.

EASY ENCHILADA SAUCE

TOTAL TIME 15 MINUTES

THE INGREDIENTS

- Fresh cilantro leaves - ⅓ cup
- Mild or medium salsa verde – 3 cups
- Heavy cream – ¼ cup

INGREDIENTS FOR 4-6 SERVINGS

METHOD

1. Add the cilantro and salsa verde to a blender and blitz until smooth.
2. Pour the mixture into a skillet over moderate heat and bring to a simmer while stirring for 6-7 minutes until the mixture reduces by two-thirds.
3. Stir the heavy cream into the sauce until combined.
4. Take the skillet off the heat and use the sauce straight away.
5. Alternatively, allow the sauce to cool and store in the refrigerator for up to 5 days.

COLA BBQ SAUCE

THE INGREDIENTS

- Ketchup – 2 cups
- Cola, any brand – 2 cups
- Worcestershire sauce – ½ cup
- Garlic powder – ¾ teaspoon
- Onion powder – ¾ teaspoon
- Freshly ground black pepper – ¾ teaspoon
- Light brown sugar – ¼ cup
- Freshly squeezed lemon juice – 2 tablespoons

METHOD

1. In a saucepan, over low heat, combine the ketchup, cola, Worcestershire sauce, garlic powder, onion powder, black pepper, brown sugar, and freshly squeezed lemon juice.
2. Bring the mixture to simmer while occasionally stirring for 15 minutes.
3. Use as needed.

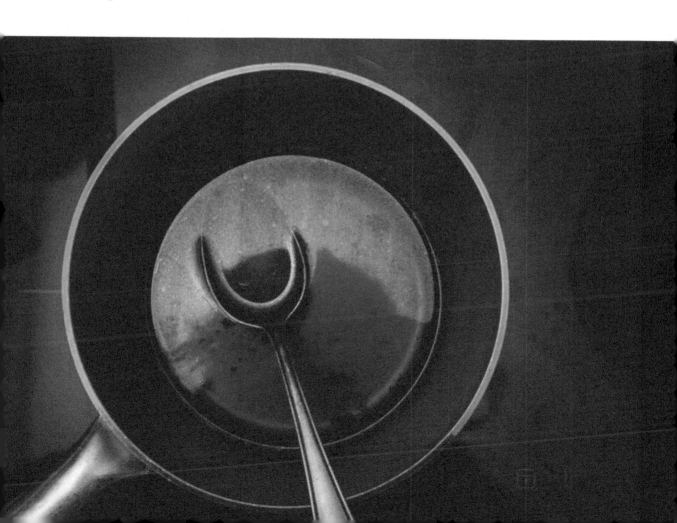

CHERRY BBQ SAUCE

THE INGREDIENTS

INGREDIENTS FOR 3½ CUPS

METHOD

* Fresh sweet cherries, stemmed and pitted – 2 cups
* Water, divided - ⅔ cup + 1 tablespoon
* Brown sugar – ½ cup
* Tomato paste – 1 tablespoon
* Balsamic vinegar – 3 tablespoons
* Garlic, peeled and minced – 1 teaspoon
* Salt
* A pinch of red chili flakes
* Cornstarch – 1 tablespoon

1. Combine the cherries, ⅔ cup water, sugar, tomato paste, balsamic vinegar, garlic, salt, and red pepper flakes in a pot. Over moderate to high heat, bring to a boil. Turn the heat down to moderate heat and simmer until the fruit is softened and the sauce is reduced slightly. This step will take around 10 minutes.

2. Using an immersion blender, puree the cherries. Strain the puree through a fine-mesh strainer and remove and discard the skins.

3. Return the puree to the pot and bring to a simmer over moderate heat.

4. In a small bowl, combine the cornstarch with one tablespoon of water. Whisk the slurry a little at a time into the sauce until you achieve your preferred consistency.

5. Allow the sauce to cool and store in a suitable container in the fridge for no more than 3 weeks. Serve with chicken or pork.

PINEAPPLE BBQ SAUCE

TOTAL TIME 20 MINUTES

INGREDIENTS FOR 3 CUPS

THE INGREDIENTS

- Fresh pineapple juice – 1 cup + more if needed
- Reduced-sodium soy sauce – 4 tablespoons
- Tomato paste – 4 tablespoons
- Cornstarch – 2 tablespoons + more if needed
- Molasses, not blackstrap – 1 tablespoon
- Runny honey – 2 tablespoons
- Sesame oil – 1 tablespoon
- Worcestershire sauce – 1 teaspoon
- Ground ginger – 1 teaspoon
- Dried garlic powder – 1 teaspoon
- Fresh pineapple, peeled, cored, and finely diced – 1 cup

METHOD

1. Off the heat source, combine the pineapple juice with the soy sauce, tomato paste, cornstarch, molasses, honey, sesame oil, Worcestershire sauce, ginger, garlic powder. Whisk until lump-free.
2. Place on the heat, stir in the diced pineapple, and bring to a boil while continually whisking.
3. Reduce the heat to a simmer and while stirring, cook until thickened. You may add more pineapple juice if the sauce is too thick. Alternatively, if it is too thin, whisk a small amount of cornstarch combined with a drop of cold pineapple juice, and whisk into the sauce.
4. Pour the sauce into a jar while hot and cool before sealing with a tight-fitting lid and storing it in the refrigerator.
5. Use as needed with meat, poultry, or fish.

SPICY MEXICAN CARAMEL GLAZE

CHAPTER 2

GLAZES

PEACH BARBECUE GLAZE

TOTAL TIME 45 MINUTES

INGREDIENTS FOR 4 CUPS

THE INGREDIENTS

- 4 ripe peaches, peeled, pitted, and pureed
- White vinegar – 1 cup
- Vegetable oil – ¼ cup
- 1 garlic cloves, peeled and crushed
- Freshly squeezed lemon juice – 3 tablespoons
- Worcestershire sauce – 1 tablespoon
- Ground ginger – ¼ teaspoon
- Black pepper – ½ teaspoon
- Dijon mustard – 1 tablespoon
- Corn syrup – ¾ cup
- Ground cinnamon – 1 teaspoon
- Light brown sugar – 1 cup

METHOD

1. In a large pan, combine the peach puree with the white vinegar, vegetable oil, garlic, lemon juice. Worcestershire sauce, ground ginger, black pepper, mustard, corn syrup, cinnamon, and light brown sugar. Heat the mixture to a low boil, and continue to simmer while frequently stirring for 30 minutes.
2. Use the glaze to baste pork, chicken, or ham.

BANANA KETCHUP GLAZE FOR CHICKEN WINGS

TOTAL TIME 5 MINUTES

INGREDIENTS FOR ½ CUP

THE INGREDIENTS

- Banana ketchup – ¼ cup
- Apple cider vinegar – 1 tablespoon
- Liquid aminos – 1 tablespoon
- Extra virgin olive oil – 1 tablespoon

METHOD

1. Combine the banana ketchup, apple cider vinegar, liquid aminos, and olive oil in a bowl. Stir to incorporate and brush over chicken wings.
2. Enjoy.

SPICY MEXICAN CARAMEL GLAZE

TOTAL COOK TIME 20 MINUTES

INGREDIENTS FOR 4½ CUPS

THE INGREDIENTS

- Piloncillo, grated (8-ozs, 227-gms)
- Water – 1½ teaspoons
- Granulated sugar – ½ cup
- Dried hibiscus flower – 1½ cups
- Achiote paste – 1 tablespoon
- Cider vinegar – 2 tablespoons
- Pinch salt

METHOD

1. Add the piloncillo, water, and sugar to a saucepan over low heat. Bring to a simmer and cook until the sugar dissolves, stirring frequently.
2. Take off the heat and stir in the dried hibiscus flower followed by the achiote paste, cider vinegar, and salt. Return the pan to the heat and simmer for 8-10 minutes until thick and caramel-like.
3. Allow the glaze to cool before transferring to a resealable jar. Keep chilled for up to 28 days.

MINT JELLY GLAZE FOR ROAST LAMB

TOTAL TIME 5 MINUTES

INGREDIENTS FOR ⅗ CUP

THE INGREDIENTS

- Mint jelly – ½ cup
- Brown sugar – 2 tablespoons
- Wholegrain mustard – 1 tablespoon

METHOD

1. Combine the mint jelly with brown sugar and wholegrain mustard in a small pan over moderate heat in a bowl. Cook, while stirring for 2 minutes, until the jelly is melted and the mixture is smooth.
2. Use the lamb as a glaze for roast lamb.

BLACKBERRY GLAZE

TOTAL TIME 10 MINUTES

THE INGREDIENTS

- Blackberry preserves – ½ cup
- Red wine vinegar – ¼ cup

INGREDIENTS FOR ¾ CUP

METHOD

1. In a small saucepan, combine the blackberry preserves with red wine vinegar. Then, while stirring constantly and over moderate heat, cook until the preserves melt.
2. Remove the pan from the heat, and use to glaze as directed.

BOURBON GLAZE FOR TURKEY

TOTAL TIME 10 MINUTES

THE INGREDIENTS

- Brown sugar (5.3-oz, 150-gm)
- Bourbon whiskey – ⅗ cup
- Soy sauce – 2 tablespoons
- Butter (1-oz, 22-gm)
- Smoked paprika – 2 teaspoons

INGREDIENTS FOR ¾ CUP

METHOD

1. In a small saucepan, combine the brown sugar, bourbon, and soy sauce, and cook until the liquid has reduced by 50 percent and is not quite syrup-like.
2. Then stir in the butter and paprika, and use as directed.

WHOLEGRAIN MUSTARD MARINADE

CHAPTER 3

MARINADES

CHILI PEPPER LIME MARINADE FOR LAMB SKEWERS

TOTAL TIME 10 MINUTES

INGREDIENTS FOR ¼ CUP

THE INGREDIENTS

- 2 green chilies, seeded and coarsely chopped
- 3 garlic cloves, peeled and coarsely chopped
- Cracked black peppercorns – ½ teaspoon
- Ground cinnamon – ½ teaspoon
- Ground cardamom – ½ teaspoon
- Freshly squeezed juice of 2 limes
- Vegetable oil – 1 tablespoon

METHOD

1. Process the green chilies, garlic, black peppercorns, cinnamon, cardamom, fresh lime juice, and vegetable oil in a food blender.
2. Transfer the marinade to a bowl, cover with kitchen wrap, and transfer to the refrigerator for 1-4 hours.
3. This marinade is enough for 6-8 lamb skewers.
4. Use as needed.

APPLE MARINADE FOR BEEF

THE INGREDIENTS

- Extra-virgin olive oil – 1 tablespoon
- Lemongrass, chopped – ¼ cup
- 1 Granny Smith apple, cored and cubed
- Small chunk fresh ginger, peeled and sliced
- 3 garlic cloves, peeled and minced
- 1 red finger chile, deseeded and thinly sliced
- 3 star anise
- Soy sauce – ¼ cup
- Water – ½ cup
- Apple juice – 3 tablespoons
- Brown sugar – 1 tablespoon
- Rice wine vinegar – 1 tablespoon

METHOD

1. Warm the oil in a saucepan over moderate heat. Add the lemongrass, apple, ginger, garlic, chile, and star anise to the pan and sauté for 5 minutes while stirring.
2. Add the soy sauce, water, apple juice, brown sugar, and vinegar to the pan and stir. Bring the mixture to a simmer.
3. Take the pan off the heat and allow it to cool for 5 minutes before using it as a marinade.

WHOLEGRAIN MUSTARD MARINADE

THE INGREDIENTS

- Wholegrain mustard– 3 tablespoons
- Freshly squeezed juice of 1 lemon
- Olive oil – 2 tablespoons
- Honey – 1 tablespoon
- White wine vinegar – 1 tablespoon
- Thyme leaves – 1 teaspoon

METHOD

1. In a bowl, combine the mustard with lemon juice, olive oil, honey, white wine vinegar, and thyme leaves.
2. Use as needed as a marinade for veggies or meat.
3. Enjoy.

SPICY PINK GRAPEFRUIT AND HERB MARINADE FOR FISH

TOTAL TIME 10 MINUTES

INGREDIENTS FOR 4 SERVINGS

THE INGREDIENTS

- 1 large pink grapefruit
- Olive oil – ¼ cup
- Honey – 2 tablespoons
- Soy sauce – 3 tablespoons
- Fresh basil, chopped – 1 tablespoon
- Fresh rosemary, chopped – 1 tablespoon
- Red pepper flakes, crushed - ⅛ teaspoon
- 2 garlic cloves, peeled and chopped

METHOD

1. Use a zester to grate 1 teaspoon of zest from the grapefruit and add to a bowl. Cut the grapefruit in half and squeeze the juice from the fruit into the bowl with the zest.
2. To the same bowl, add the oil, honey, soy sauce, basil, rosemary, red pepper flakes, and garlic. Stir to combine and pour over your choice of fish.
3. For best results, allow the marinade to soak for at least an hour.

CORONATION CURRY MARINADE

PEANUT AND GINGER MARINADE

TOTAL COOK TIME 20 MINUTES

INGREDIENTS FOR 2 CUPS

THE INGREDIENTS

- Hot water – ½ cup
- Smooth peanut butter – ½ cup
- Chili paste – ¼ cup
- Soy sauce – ¼ cup
- White vinegar – 2 tablespoons
- Vegetable oil – 2 tablespoons
- 4 garlic cloves, peeled and minced
- Red pepper flakes – ¼ teaspoon
- Small chunk fresh ginger, grated

METHOD

1. In a bowl, stir together the hot water and peanut butter until the peanut butter has melted. Next, stir in the chili paste, soy sauce, vinegar, vegetable oil, garlic, red pepper flakes, and ginger.
2. Add your choice of meat to the marinade and toss to coat. Cover and chill overnight before cooking.

CORONATION CURRY MARINADE

TOTAL TIME 5 MINUTES

INGREDIENTS FOR ½ CUP

THE INGREDIENTS

- Medium curry powder – 1 tablespoon
- Fresh lime juice – 2 tablespoons
- Finely grated zest of ½ lime
- Natural yogurt – 3 tablespoons
- Mango chutney – 1 tablespoon
- Sunflower oil – 1 tablespoon
- Coriander, finely chopped – 1 tablespoon

METHOD

1. Combine the curry powder with lime juice, lime zest, natural yogurt, mango chutney, sunflower oil, and coriander in a bowl.
2. Use the marinade as needed.

KOREAN BBQ RUB

CHAPTER 4

WET RUBS

MUSTARD-ORANGE RUB

TOTAL TIME 10 MINUTES

THE INGREDIENTS

- Dijon mustard – 2 cups
- Fresh parsley, minced – 1 cup
- Dried orange peel – ½ cup
- Rosemary leaves, crushed – ½ cup
- Black pepper – ¼ cup
- Salt – 1 tablespoon

INGREDIENTS FOR 18 SERVINGS

METHOD

1. Combine the mustard, parsley, orange peel, rosemary leaves, black pepper, and salt.
2. Use as directed.

KOREAN BBQ RUB

TOTAL TIME 4 MINUTES

THE INGREDIENTS

- Packed brown sugar – ¼ cup
- Salt – 1 teaspoon
- Reduced-sodium soy sauce – 2 teaspoons
- Dark sesame oil – 2 teaspoons
- 4 garlic cloves, peeled and minced

INGREDIENTS FOR ⅓ CUP

METHOD

1. In a bowl, combine the brown sugar with the salt, soy sauce, sesame oil, and garlic.
2. Use the wet rub before grilling for game birds, steak, tenderloin, salmon fillets, and dark meat chicken.
3. Transfer any unused rub to an airtight container and store in the fridge for up to 7 days.

MAPLE SAGE SPICE RUB

MAPLE SAGE SPICE RUB

TOTAL TIME 5 MINUTES

THE INGREDIENTS

- Kosher salt - 4 tablespoons
- Dried sage, crumbled – 2 tablespoons
- Pumpkin pie spice – ½ teaspoon
- Coarsely ground black pepper – ½ teaspoon
- Garlic powder – ½ teaspoon
- Dark maple syrup – 2 tablespoons

INGREDIENTS FOR ⅗ CUP

METHOD

1. Combine the kosher salt, dried sage, pumpkin pie spice, black pepper, and garlic powder in a small bowl. Add the maple syrup and stir the mixture thoroughly.

2. Use as needed.

ORANGE-SAGE RUB FOR MEAT, POULTRY, AND FISH

TOTAL TIME 10 MINUTES

THE INGREDIENTS

- Orange zest, freshly grated – 1 tablespoon
- 3 garlic cloves, peeled and finely minced
- Fresh sage, finely minced – 1 tablespoon
- Extra-virgin olive oil – 1 tablespoon
- Honey – 1 tablespoon
- Freshly ground black pepper – ¼ teaspoon
- Salt – ¼ teaspoon

INGREDIENTS FOR 5-6 TABLESPOONS

METHOD

1. Combine the orange zest, garlic, sage, oil, honey, black pepper, and salt in a bowl.

2. Use as directed.

SMOKEY 'N SPICY CHILI LIME WET RUB

TOTAL TIME 10 MINUTES

INGREDIENTS FOR 6 TABLESPOONS

THE INGREDIENTS

- Kosher salt – 2 tablespoons
- Lime zest, finely chopped – 1 tablespoon
- Chili powder – 1 tablespoon
- Smoked paprika – ½ tablespoon
- Dried cilantro – 1 teaspoon
- Onion powder – ½ teaspoon
- Garlic powder – ½ teaspoon
- Olive oil – 3 tablespoons

METHOD

1. Combine the kosher salt, lime zest, chili powder, smoked paprika, dried cilantro, onion powder, garlic powder, and olive oil in a small bowl. Stir to incorporate and transfer to the fridge until ready to use.
2. Use as directed.

WET RUB FOR RIBS

MULTI-PURPOSE WET RUB

THE INGREDIENTS

- Brown sugar – ¼ cup
- Salt – 1 teaspoon
- Soy sauce – 2 teaspoons
- Dark sesame oil – 2 teaspoons
- 4 garlic cloves, peeled and minced

METHOD

1. Combine all the ingredients (brown sugar, salt, soy sauce, sesame oil, and garlic) in an airtight container, stirring to incorporate. Seal with a lid and transfer to the fridge until needed.
2. Serve as needed with meat, fish or poultry.

WET RUB FOR RIBS

THE INGREDIENTS

- Brown sugar – ½ cup
- Ground cumin – 1 tablespoon
- Ancho chile powder – 1 tablespoon
- Smoked paprika – 1 tablespoon
- Garlic salt – 1 tablespoon
- Balsamic vinegar – 3 tablespoons
- Apple juice – 2 cups

METHOD

1. In a bowl, combine all of the ingredients (brown sugar, ground cumin, ancho chili powder, smoked paprika, garlic salt, balsamic vinegar, and apple juice).
2. Brush the ribs all over on both sides with the rub and allow to rest for a minimum of 10 minutes before cooking.

ALL-PURPOSE DRY RUB

CHAPTER 5

DRY RUBS

ASIAN DRY RUB

TOTAL TIME 5 MINUTES
THE INGREDIENTS

- Dried basil – 4 teaspoons
- Dried mint – 4 teaspoons
- Salt – 2 teaspoons
- Ground ginger – 2 teaspoons
- Paprika – 2 teaspoons
- Ground red pepper – 1½ teaspoons
- Freshly ground black pepper – 1 teaspoon
- Garlic powder – ½ teaspoon

INGREDIENTS FOR ½ CUP
METHOD

1. In a Mason jar, combine all the ingredients (dried basil, dried mint, salt, ground ginger, paprika, red pepper, black pepper, and garlic powder).
2. Seal the jar with its lid, and store for up to 14 days.
3. Use as needed.

FESTIVE MEAT RUB

TOTAL TIME 5 MINUTES
THE INGREDIENTS

- Garlic powder – 3 tablespoons
- Dried onion flakes – 3 tablespoons
- Ground cinnamon – 3 tablespoons
- Smoked paprika – 1 tablespoon

INGREDIENTS FOR ⅓ CUP
METHOD

1. Add the garlic powder, dried onion flakes, cinnamon, smoked paprika, and shake to combine in a Mason jar.
2. Seal the lid and use as directed.

MEDITERRANEAN RUB

TOTAL TIME 3 MINUTES
THE INGREDIENTS

- Ground sage – 2 teaspoons
- Dry thyme – 2 teaspoons
- Black pepper – 2 teaspoons
- Salt – 1 teaspoon
- Garlic powder – 1 teaspoon
- Dried rosemary, crushed – 1 teaspoon

INGREDIENTS FOR ⅓ CUP
METHOD

1. In a bowl, combine ground sage with the dry thyme, black pepper, salt, garlic powder, and dried rosemary.
2. Use as a rub for beef steak, lamb, or chicken.
3. Store any unused rub in a suitable container.

ALL-PURPOSE DRY RUB

TOTAL COOK TIME 8 MINUTES
THE INGREDIENTS

- Packed brown sugar – ¾ cup
- Sea salt – 3 tablespoons
- Paprika – 3 tablespoons
- Chili powder – 3 tablespoons
- Onion powder – 2 tablespoons
- Garlic powder – 2 tablespoons
- Ground cumin – 1 tablespoon
- Dried oregano – 1 tablespoon

INGREDIENTS FOR 1½ CUPS
METHOD

1. Add all the ingredients (packed brown sugar, sea salt, paprika, chili powder, onion powder, garlic powder, ground cumin, and dried oregano) to a bowl and combine.
2. Transfer to an airtight container and store in a cool, dry environment for up to 12 months.
3. Use as and when needed.

SPICE RUB FOR SHRIMP

TOTAL TIME 8 MINUTES

INGREDIENTS FOR ⅛ CUP

THE INGREDIENTS

- Garlic powder – 1 teaspoon
- Sweet paprika – 1 teaspoon
- Dried basil – 1 teaspoon
- Smoked paprika – 1 teaspoon
- Dried oregano – 1 teaspoon
- Ground cumin – 1 teaspoon
- Onion powder – 1 teaspoon
- Salt and black pepper to season
- A dash of cayenne pepper

METHOD

1. Combine the garlic powder, sweet paprika, dried basil, smoked paprika, dried oregano, ground cumin, and onion powder in a small bowl. Season with salt, black pepper, and a dash of cayenne.
2. Transfer to an airtight resealable container at room temperature.
3. Use the spice rub as directed.

GINGER RUB

THE INGREDIENTS

- Ground ginger – 2 tablespoons
- Dried crushed red pepper – ½ teaspoon
- Salt – 1 teaspoon
- Black pepper – 1 teaspoon

METHOD

1. In a small bowl, combine the ingredients (ground ginger, dried crushed red pepper, salt, and black pepper).
2. To use: Scatter the rub generously over your choice of protein before cooking.
3. Store any unused rub in a suitable airtight container in a cool environment.

ITALIAN SEASONING

CHAPTER 6

SEASONINGS

CREOLE SEASONING

THE INGREDIENTS

METHOD

- Paprika – 2 tablespoons + 1½ teaspoons
- Garlic powder – 2 tablespoons
- Salt – 1 tablespoon
- Onion powder – 1 tablespoon
- Dried oregano – 1 tablespoon
- Dried thyme – 1 tablespoon
- Cayenne pepper – 1 tablespoon
- Pepper – 1 tablespoon

1. Add all the ingredients (paprika, garlic powder, salt, onion powder, dried oregano, dried thyme, cayenne pepper, and pepper) to a bowl and combine.

2. Transfer to an airtight container and store in a cool, dry environment for up to 12 months.

3. Use as and when needed for seafood, veggies, chicken, and red meat.

MIXED MUSHROOM SEASONING

TOTAL TIME 10 MINUTES

INGREDIENTS FOR ½ CUP

THE INGREDIENTS

- Dried ground porcini mushrooms – 3 tablespoons
- Dried ground morel mushrooms – 3 tablespoons
- Coarse salt – 2 teaspoons
- Freshly ground white pepper – ¼ teaspoon
- Dried thyme – 1½ teaspoons
- Lemon zest, finely chopped – 1 tablespoon

METHOD

1. Pulse the porcini and morel mushrooms until coarsely ground in a food processor.
2. Then add the salt, white pepper, thyme, and lemon zest. Pulse the seasoning until fine.
3. Transfer the seasoning to a small airtight resealable container and store for up to 28 days.

ITALIAN SEASONING

TOTAL COOK TIME 5 MINUTES

INGREDIENTS FOR ½ CUP

THE INGREDIENTS

- Basil – 4 teaspoons
- Marjoram – 4 teaspoons
- Garlic powder – 2 teaspoons
- Rosemary – 4 teaspoons
- Oregano – 4 teaspoons
- Savory – 4 teaspoons
- Thyme – 4 teaspoons

METHOD

1. Add all the ingredients (basil, marjoram, garlic powder, rosemary, oregano, savory, and thyme) to a bowl and combine.
2. Transfer to an airtight container.
3. Stir before use.

SWEET 'N SMOKEY SEASONING FOR SALMON

TOTAL TIME 5 MINUTES

INGREDIENTS FOR ¼ CUP

THE INGREDIENTS

- Brown sugar – 2 tablespoons
- Black pepper – 2 teaspoons
- Coarse ground sea salt – 1 teaspoon
- Dried basil – ½ teaspoon
- Garlic powder – ½ teaspoon
- Smoked paprika – ½ teaspoon

METHOD

1. In a bowl, combine the brown sugar with the black pepper, sea salt, dried basil, garlic powder, and smoked paprika. With a whisk or metal fork, stir to break up any lumps and until blended.
2. Scatter the seasoning liberally over a salmon fillet of up to (2-lbs, 0.9-kgs) in weight and cook to your preference.

LIME TACO SEASONING

TOTAL TIME 5 MINUTES

THE INGREDIENTS

- Chili powder – 4 tablespoons
- Cumin – 2 tablespoons
- Garlic powder – 1 teaspoon
- Paprika – 2 teaspoons
- Coarse kosher salt – 1 tablespoon
- Lime pepper – 2 teaspoons
- Onion powder – 1 teaspoon
- Ground coriander – ½ teaspoon

INGREDIENTS FOR ⅗ CUP

METHOD

1. In a Mason jar, combine all the ingredients (chili powder, cumin, garlic powder, paprika, kosher salt, lime pepper, onion powder, and ground coriander).
2. Store in an airtight container and use approximately 2 tablespoons of the mixture per (1-lb, 0.5-kg) of meat.

SWEET AND SPICY APRICOT BASTING SAUCE

CHAPTER 7

BASTES AND BRINES

HONEY SOY BASTE FOR PORK CHOPS

TOTAL TIME 15 MINUTES

INGREDIENTS FOR ⅛ CUP

THE INGREDIENTS

- Honey – 1 tablespoon
- Dijon mustard – 1 tablespoon
- Soy sauce – 1 tablespoon
- 1 garlic clove, peeled and minced

METHOD

1. Combine the honey, Dijon mustard, soy sauce, and garlic in a small bowl. Stir to incorporate.
2. Use the baste for pork chops while basting frequently.
3. This recipe is enough for 4 pork chops.

SWEET AND SPICY APRICOT BASTING SAUCE

TOTAL TIME 20 MINUTES

INGREDIENTS FOR 2 CUPS

THE INGREDIENTS

- Apricot jam – 1 cup
- White vinegar – ½ cup
- Worcestershire sauce – 3 tablespoons
- Dijon mustard – 2 tablespoons
- Honey – 2 tablespoons
- Crushed red pepper – 2 teaspoons

METHOD

1. In a small pan, combine the apricot jam, white vinegar, Worcestershire sauce, Dijon mustard, honey, and red pepper. Heat over moderate heat until the jam and honey melt.
2. Brush the baste over the meat at the end of the grilling process.

BRINE FOR SMOKED SALMON

TOTAL TIME 10 MINUTES

INGREDIENTS FOR 20+ CUPS

THE INGREDIENTS

- Water – 16 cups
- Kosher salt – 1 cup
- White sugar – 1 cup
- Brown sugar – 1 cup
- Lemon pepper, to season
- 1 package dry seafood seasoning mix (3-oz,85-gm)
- Freshly ground black pepper to season
- 4 garlic cloves, peeled and crushed
- A dash of hot pepper sauce to season
- 4 fresh lemons, peeled, sliced, seeded, and crushed
- 2 fresh oranges, peeled, seeded, sliced, and crushed
- 1 fresh lime, peeled, seeded, sliced, and crushed
- 1 large onion, peeled and sliced

METHOD

1. Pour the water into a small bucket. Add the kosher salt, white and brown sugars, lemon pepper, seafood seasoning, and black pepper. Then, add the garlic, hot pepper sauce, crushed lemon, crushed orange, crushed lime, and onion.
2. To use, soak the salmon in the brine in the fridge for 12-36 hours. Then, smoke the salmon as directed.

BASTE FOR GRILLED FISH

THE INGREDIENTS

METHOD

- Butter – ¼ cup
- Brown sugar – ¼ cup
- Powdered garlic – 1 teaspoon
- Fresh lemon juice – 2 tablespoons
- Soy sauce – ½ -1 tablespoon, as needed
- Black pepper – 1 teaspoon
- A pinch of cayenne pepper

1. In a small saucepan, combine the butter, brown sugar, garlic, lemon juice, soy sauce (to taste), black pepper, and a pinch of cayenne. Over low heat, cook until the sugar dissolves. Set aside to cool.
2. Use as directed.

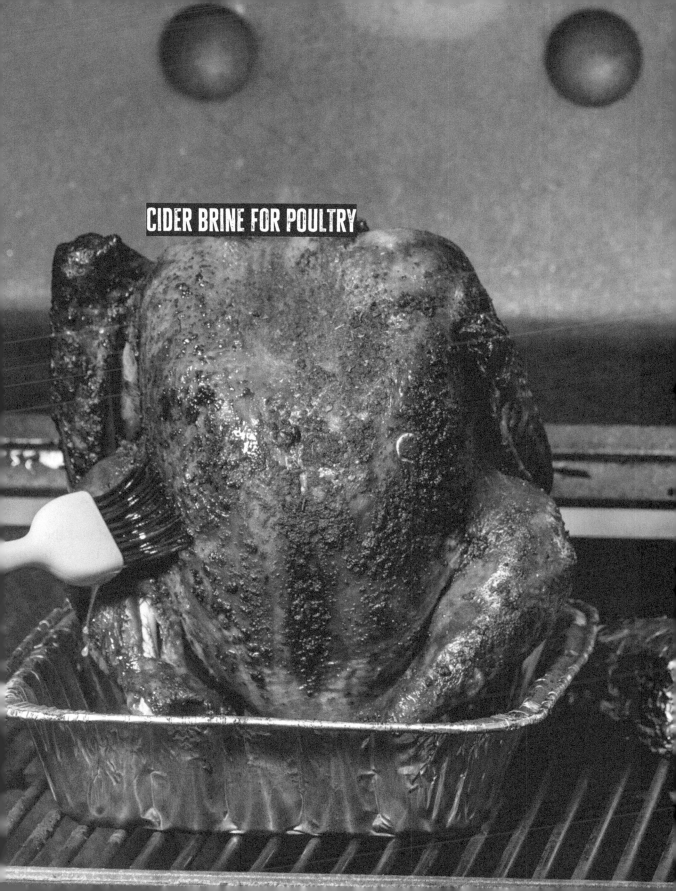

CIDER BRINE FOR POULTRY

BUTTER SAUCE AND BASTE FOR SEAFOOD

TOTAL TIME 10 MINUTES

INGREDIENTS FOR ½ CUP

THE INGREDIENTS

- Butter, cubed – ½ cup
- Dried rosemary, crushed – ½ teaspoon
- Dried tarragon – ½ teaspoon
- Salt – ¾ teaspoon
- Fresh lemon juice – 1 tablespoon

METHOD

1. Combine the butter, rosemary, tarragon, salt, and lemon juice in a small saucepan. Over low heat, cook until the butter melts. Set aside to cool.
2. Use as directed.

CIDER BRINE FOR POULTRY

TOTAL TIME 15 MINUTES

INGREDIENTS FOR 12-14 SERVINGS

THE INGREDIENTS

- Hard cider – 8 cups
- Apple cider – 4 cups
- Water, room temperature – 4 cups
- Kosher salt – 1½ cups
- Black peppercorns – 2 tablespoons
- A thumb of fresh ginger, peeled and sliced
- 2 fresh lemons, sliced
- 6 sprigs each of fresh thyme and rosemary
- Ice water – 6 cups

METHOD

1. Combine the hard cider, apple cider, water, salt, black peppercorns, ginger, sliced lemon, thyme, and rosemary sprigs in a large saucepan. Over moderate heat, bring to a boil and stir until the salt dissolves.
2. Remove the pan from the heat, and add the water. Allow to completely cool to room temperature.

MEMPHIS MOP FOR RIBS

CHAPTER 8

MOPS AND BUTTERS

CAROLINA MOPPING SAUCE

THE INGREDIENTS

- Distilled white vinegar – 1 cup
- Cider vinegar – 1 cup
- Red pepper flakes – 1 tablespoon
- Hot sauce – 1 tablespoon
- Garlic powder – 1 teaspoon
- Onion powder – 1 teaspoon
- Packed brown sugar – 2 tablespoons
- Dry mustard – 1 teaspoon
- Salt – ½ teaspoon
- Ground black pepper – ¼ teaspoon

METHOD

1. Combine the white vinegar, cider vinegar, red pepper flakes, hot sauce, garlic powder, onion powder, brown sugar, dry mustard, salt, and black pepper in a bowl.
2. Transfer to an airtight resealable container and store in the fridge for up to 28 days.
3. Use as directed.

MEMPHIS MOP FOR RIBS

THE INGREDIENTS

- Apple cider vinegar – 2 cups
- Water – 1 cup
- Memphis rub – ¼ cup
- BBQ sauce, any brand – ¼ cup

METHOD

1. Combine the apple cider vinegar, water, rub, and BBQ sauce in a bowl.
2. Stir well to incorporate and use as directed.

GARLIC BUTTER BBQ SAUCE FOR SHRIMP

BUTTER BBQ SAUCE

THE INGREDIENTS

- Butter – ½ cup
- Onion, peeled and chopped – ½ cup
- Catsup – ½ cup
- Worcestershire sauce – 3 tablespoons
- Firmly packed light brown sugar – ¼ cup
- Chili powder – 1½ teaspoons
- Salt – 1 teaspoon
- Black pepper - ⅛ teaspoon
- Tabasco sauce, as needed, to taste

METHOD

1. In a pan, melt the butter.
2. Add the onion to the melted butter, and cook until tender.
3. Add the catsup, Worcestershire sauce, brown sugar, chili powder, salt, black pepper, and Tabasco sauce, to taste. Stir the sauce to combine and simmer for approximately 5 minutes.
4. Serve.

GARLIC BUTTER BBQ SAUCE FOR SHRIMP

THE INGREDIENTS

- Unsalted butter – ½ cup
- 4 garlic cloves, peeled and minced
- 1 shallot, minced
- Crushed red pepper flakes – ¼ teaspoon
- Sea salt and black pepper, to season, as needed

METHOD

1. In a small skillet, melt the butter over moderate heat.
2. Stir in the garlic, shallot, and red pepper flakes until fragrant for approximately 2 minutes. Season the sauce with sea salt and black pepper to taste.
3. Use the sauce to baste the shrimp.

BBQ BEEF COFFEE CURE

CHAPTER 9

CURES

BBQ BEEF COFFEE CURE

TOTAL TIME 10 MINUTES

INGREDIENTS FOR 2½ CUPS

THE INGREDIENTS

- Dark roast coffee, finely ground - ⅓ cup
- Dark chili powder - ⅓ cup
- Smoked paprika - ⅓ cup
- Kosher salt – ½ cup
- Packed dark brown sugar - ⅔ cup
- Sugar – 3 tablespoons
- Granulated garlic – 2 tablespoons
- Ground cumin – 1 tablespoon
- Cayenne pepper – 1 teaspoon

METHOD

1. In a bowl, combine the dark roast coffee, chili powder, paprika, kosher salt, brown sugar, sugar, garlic, cumin, and cayenne pepper, and break up any clumps with clean hands.
2. Transfer to an airtight resealable container in a cool, dry environment.
3. Use as directed.

CHIPOTLE CORINADER CURE FOR SPARERIBS

TOTAL TIME 10 MINUTES

INGREDIENTS FOR 2½-3 CUPS

THE INGREDIENTS

- Coriander seeds – ¼ cup
- Black peppercorns – ¼ cup
- 8 garlic cloves, peeled
- 4 shallots, peeled
- Chipotle chili – ¼ cup
- Ketchup – 1 cup
- Molasses – ¼ cup
- Cider vinegar – ¼ cup
- Packed brown sugar – 6 tablespoons
- Orange zest, finely minced – 1 tablespoon

METHOD

1. Add the coriander and black peppercorns to a small dry frying pan over moderate heat, and toast until the peppercorns start to smoke. Transfer to a spice grinder and grind to a fine consistency.
2. In a food processor, mince the garlic. Add the ground spices, shallots, chipotle chilies, and mince for 8-10 seconds.
3. Add the remaining cure ingredients (ketchup, molasses, cider vinegar, brown sugar, and orange zest) and process to a thick paste-like consistency.
4. Use as per your recipe instructions.

DUCK CURE

DUCK CURE

THE INGREDIENTS

- Brown sugar (3.5-oz, 100-gm)
- Coarse salt (4.6-oz, 130-gm)
- Sichuan peppercorns, crushed – 2 teaspoons
- Fennel seeds, crushed – 1 teaspoon

INGREDIENTS FOR 1¼ CUPS

METHOD

1. Combine the brown sugar, coarse salt, Sichuan peppercorns, and fennel seeds in a bowl.
2. To use, spread around ⅓ of the cure in the bottom of a dish that is a snug fit for the duck. Place the duck fillet skin side facing up and completely cover the remaining cure. Cover with kitchen wrap and transfer to the fridge for 72 hours.
3. Use as directed in your recipe.

FISH CURE

THE INGREDIENTS

- Coarse sea salt (8.8-oz, 250-gm)
- Sugar (8.8-oz, 250-gm)
- Zest of 2 lemons
- Zest of 1 lime

INGREDIENTS FOR 2½ CUPS

METHOD

1. Combine the salt, sugar, lemon zest, and lime zest in a bowl. Stir to incorporate and spread half of the cure onto a large rimmed tray.
2. Set the fish on top of the cure, and pour over the remaining cure. Cover with kitchen wrap, and place in the fridge for 12 hours.
3. Prepare the fish as needed.

BROWN SUGAR CURE FOR SALMON

TOTAL TIME 10 MINUTES

INGREDIENTS FOR 8-12 SERVINGS

THE INGREDIENTS

- Brown sugar (12.5-lb, 5.7-kg)
- Kosher salt (4.5-lb, 2-kg)
- Coarsely ground black pepper (0.5-lb, 227-gm)
- Red pepper flakes (3.25-oz, 92-gm)
- Fennel seeds (7-oz, 198-gm)
- 2 bunches of fresh dill

METHOD

1. Combine the brown sugar, salt, black pepper, red pepper flakes, fennel seeds, and fresh dill in a bowl. Mix thoroughly to combine.
2. Apply the mixture liberally to the salmon and allow the sugar to dissolve into the fish.

BEEF BRISKET

CHAPTER 10

BBQ RECIPES

BEEF BRISKET

TOTAL COOK TIME 8 HOURS 30 MINUTES

THE MEAT

- 1 whole beef brisket, untrimmed (11-lb, 5-kg)

THE INGREDIENTS

- Cooking salt – 4 tablespoons
- Black pepper – 1 tablespoon
- BBQ sauce, of choice – 2 cups

THE BBQ

- Preheat the BBQ to 230°F (110°C) and prepare for indirect cooking
- Put a few handfuls of mesquite and oak wood on the BBQ. When smoke appears, you are ready to cook
- After 1 hour of cooking, add another few handfuls of mesquite and oak wood to the BBQ

METHOD

1. Use a sharp knife to trim the fat right down on the fatty side of the brisket. On the meatier side, cut away the membrane until the grainy meat below is visible. Remove any remaining clumps of fat.

INGREDIENTS FOR 10 SERVINGS

2. In a small bowl, combine the salt and black pepper and season the brisket all over with it.

3. Spritz the brisket with water on both sides. When the BBQ is smoking, place the brisket on the cooking grate fat side down and close the lid. Cook for 4 hours over indirect heat. At this point, the brisket should have developed a dark outer crust, and the internal temperature should be 160°F (70°C) at the thickest part.

4. Take the brisket off the BBQ and spray it all over with more water. Next, wrap the brisket in a sheet of baking paper and then tightly wrap in kitchen foil.

5. Return the wrapped brisket to the BBQ fat side down on the top grate and close the lid. Cook for another 2-4 hours over indirect heat until the internal temperature of the meat reaches 200°F (95°C). The meat should be very tender and feel very soft to the touch when pressed.

6. Take the cooked beef off the BBQ but do not unwrap. Instead, place the meat inside an insulated cool box, close the lid and allow the meat to rest for 2-4 hours.

7. Unwrap the brisket and transfer to a cutting board.

8. In a saucepan over moderate heat on the stove, warm the BBQ sauce for 5 minutes.

9. Cut the brisket across the grain into thin slices and serve with warm BBQ sauce.

PULLED PORK BUNS

THE MEAT

- Rind off pork scotch (3.3-lb, 1.5-kg)

THE INGREDIENTS

- Smoked paprika – 1 tablespoon
- Brown sugar – 2 tablespoons
- Salt – 1 teaspoon
- Onion powder – 1 teaspoon
- Garlic powder – 1 teaspoon
- Cayenne pepper – ½ teaspoon
- Ground cumin – 1 teaspoon
- Black pepper – ½ teaspoon
- ½ cup apple cider vinegar
- BBQ sauce of choice – ½ cup
- 10 soft white or brioche bun, split and toasted

THE BBQ

- Heat the BBQ to low heat and prepare for indirect cooking using a convection tray and trivet

INGREDIENTS FOR 10 SERVINGS

METHOD

1. First, prepare a rub. Combine the paprika, brown sugar, salt, onion powder, garlic powder, cayenne pepper, cumin, and black pepper in a bowl. Rub the mixture all over the sides of the pork. Cover and chill for 30 minutes in the refrigerator.
2. Take the pork out of the refrigerator and allow to stand at room temperature for half an hour.
3. Place the pork on the trivet in the BBQ and cook for 3 hours.
4. After 3 hours, transfer the pork to a large drip pan and pour over the apple cider vinegar. Cover tightly with kitchen foil and cook on the BBQ for another 1½ hours.
5. Take the pork off the BBQ and allow to rest in the drip pan, covered, for 45 minutes.
6. After resting, shred the meat using two forks into medium-sized pieces.
7. Toss the shredded pork with ½ cup BBQ sauce and serve inside toasted buns.

RACK OF LAMB

TOTAL COOK TIME 8 HOURS 20 MINUTES

THE MEAT

- 2 racks of lamb (3-lb, 1.4-kg)

THE MARINADE

- Olive oil – 4 tablespoons
- Zest of 1 lemon
- Freshly squeezed juice of 1 lemon
- 4 garlic cloves, peeled and crushed
- Rosemary washed and finely chopped – 1 tablespoon
- Salt and black pepper, to season

THE BBQ

- Preheat the BBQ to moderate heat 320°F (160°C)

INGREDIENTS FOR 6 SERVINGS

METHOD

1. Combine the olive oil, lemon zest, lemon juice, garlic, and rosemary. Season with salt and black pepper.
2. Add the lamb to a baking dish.
3. Pour the marinade over the lamb and rub it in to coat.
4. Cover the dish, and transfer the dish to the fridge overnight.
5. Remove the lamb from the marinade, lay bone side down on the BBQ and sear for 4 minutes. Flip the meat over and place on indirect heat for 15 minutes, until medium-rare.
6. Remove from the heat and set aside to rest for 10 minutes before cutting into chops.
7. Serve and enjoy.

BBQ TURKEY BREAST WITH CRANBERRY SAUCE

THE MEAT

- 8 fresh turkey fillets

THE MARINADE

- Zest of 1 lemon
- Freshly squeezed lemon juice- ¼ cup
- Light olive oil – ¼ cup
- 2 garlic cloves, peeled and crushed
- Rosemary, finely chopped – 1 tablespoon
- Sea salt flakes - ½ teaspoon
- Cracked black peppercorn – ½ teaspoon

THE INGREDIENTS

- 2 oranges, peeled and pith removed
- Cranberry sauce, ready-made, store-bought (9.7-oz, 275-gm)
- Sprigs of rosemary to garnish
- A handful of pistachio kernels, toasted and chopped

THE BBQ

- Preheat the BBQ to moderate heat
- Spritz the BBQ with nonstick oil

METHOD

1. For the marinade. Combine the lemon zest, lemon juice, olive oil, garlic, rosemary, salt, and pepper in a glass bowl. Add the turkey and turn over to coat. Cover the bowl and chill for half an hour.

2. In the meantime, hold each orange over a bowl, cut either side of the membrane, release the orange segments, and set aside. Squeeze the juice into the bowl.

3. In a pan, combine while stirring the cranberry sauce with the orange juice over low heat. Add the orange segments and heat through until warmed for 60 seconds.

4. Remove the turkey from the marinade, and cook on the BBQ for 4 minutes, each side until cooked through. Transfer to a plater, and cover with aluminum foil. Allow to rest for 8-10 minutes before thickly slicing.

5. Top the sliced turkey with sprigs of rosemary, garnish with pistachios and enjoy.

CHERRY COLA CHIKEN WINGS

CHERRY COLA CHICKEN WINGS

TOTAL COOK TIME 20 HOURS 20 MINUTES

INGREDIENTS FOR 12 SERVINGS

THE MEAT

- Chicken wings, partitioned, tips discarded (4-lb, 1.8-kg)

THE BRINE

- Cherry cola – 4¼ cups
- Kosher salt – 2 tablespoons

THE INGREDIENTS

- BBQ rub – 4 tablespoons
- Brown sugar – 4 tablespoons
- Cornstarch – 4 tablespoons

THE SMOKE

- Preheat the smoker to 150°F (65°C)
- Choose your favorite wood chips

METHOD

1. Around 18 hours before you cook the wings, add them to a ziplock bag.
2. Pour in the cherry cola and 2 tablespoons of kosher salt.
3. Remove the wings from the brine, and pat dry with kitchen paper.
4. Transfer the wings to a very large bowl.
5. Add the BBQ rub, brown sugar, and cornstarch. Toss until well and evenly covered.
6. Smoke the wings for around 2 hours.
7. Remove from the smoker and enjoy.

LOBSTER TAILS ON-SHELL

TOTAL COOK TIME 1 HOUR 15 MINUTES

THE SEAFOOD

- 6 lobster tails

THE INGREDIENTS

- Salted butter – ¼ cup
- Garlic, peeled and minced – 2 tablespoons
- Chives, minced – 1 tablespoon
- Fresh parsley, minced – 1 tablespoon
- 3 lemons, halved
- Fresh juice from 3 lemons
- Fish roe (1.4-oz, 40-gm)

THE SMOKE

- Preheat the smoker to 225°F (107°C)
- Choose your favorite wood chips

INGREDIENTS FOR 6 SERVINGS

METHOD

1. Melt the butter, add the garlic, chives, and parsley in a pan, and stir to combine.
2. Using kitchen scissors cut the top shell of the lobster tails in a straight line in the middle of the lobster tails. Stop at the tail base. Flip the tail and crack the ribs in the center of the lobster tail's bottom. Carefully flip the tail and open the shell. You can do this using your thumbs. Lift the meat up, leaving the tail base attached. Close the shell under the meat, so the lobster sits on top of the shell.
3. Spread the butter over the top of the tails.
4. Arrange the halved lemons on the preheated smoker grill and place them directly on the grill, cook for around 60 minutes.
5. Drizzle lemon juice over the tails while they smoke.
6. Serve the lobster meat hot with the garlic butter from Step 1 and the fish roe.

TUNA STEAKS

TOTAL COOK TIME 20 MINUTES

THE FISH

- 4 tuna steaks 2-in(5-cm) thick (6-8-oz, 170-227-gm) each

THE INGREDIENTS

- Canola or vegetable oil, as needed
- Sea salt and black pepper to season

THE BBQ

- Clean and oil the grate
- Prepare your BBQ to high heat
- Place the grate in position, cover and preheat for 5 minutes

INGREDIENTS FOR 4 SERVINGS

METHOD

1. First, pat the tuna dry, and brush them lightly all over with oil.
2. When you are ready to start cooking, season the fish with salt and pepper.
3. Set the tuna over the hot side of the BBQ, and cook until well seared on one side, for 1-2 minutes. Gently lift the tuna steak off the grate and flip over. Sear for 1-2 minutes until medium-rare.
4. Remove from the BBQ and serve.

SOY-GLAZED CIDER CAN DUCK

SOY-GLAZED CIDER CAN DUCK

TOTAL COOK TIME 2 HOURS 30 MINUTES

INGREDIENTS FOR 4-6 SERVINGS

THE MEAT

- 1 whole duck (2-lb, 0.9-kg)

THE INGREDIENTS

- Chinese 5 spice– 1 teaspoon
- Sea salt, as needed
- Good-quality canned cider, divided - 2 cups
- A small thumb of ginger, peeled and cut into small matchsticks
- 2 garlic cloves, peeled and finely sliced
- Sesame oil – 1 teaspoon
- Soy sauce, divided - ⅔ cup
- Runny honey – 2 tablespoons
- Sriracha – 3 tablespoons
- Sichuan pepper, crushed – 2 teaspoons
- A bunch of cilantro, to serve, optional

THE BBQ

- Light your BBQ, allow the flames to die down and the coals to become ashy white. Mound the coal up on one side

METHOD

1. Using a sharp knife, lightly score the duck skin all over and rub in the Chinese 5-spice and salt, ensuring it gets into the cut marks.
2. Set around 3 tablespoons of the cider to one side. You will need it for the sauce. Pour around half of the remaining cider into a glass.
3. Add the ginger and garlic to the cider can and pour in the oil, followed by half of the soy sauce.
4. Push the duck onto the cider can, legs down, so the bird is sitting upright with the can in the bird's cavity. Stand it upright on a baking tray on the BBQ grill, close the BBQ dome lid and cook for 60 minutes.
5. While the duck cooks, whisk the remaining soy sauce, honey, and Sriracha with the 3 tablespoons of cider set aside in Step 2.
6. Brush the sauce over the duck and cook for an additional 60 minutes, basting every 12-15 minutes, until the dark is glossy and dark.
7. Remove from the BBQ and allow to rest for half an hour.
8. In the meantime, mix the Sichuan pepper with some sea falt.
9. Lift the duck carefully off the baking tray and the can. Season with the spiced salt and add the cilantro to the bird's cavity.
10. Carve the duck and enjoy.

CHAPTER 11

BBQ SAUCES TIPS

BBQ SAUCE INGREDIENTS

BBQ sauces can be made by using many types of ingredients and even techniques. But almost all of them contain few reoccurring ingredients that are universally used for making these sauces. The complement the meat, elevating their flavor profile and making the dishes even more lip-smacking. Here is the list of the most commonly used ingredients for BBQ sauces.

- Ketchup: It usually makes the base of the sauce. It has sweet notes, but you should avoid ketchup made by corn syrup.

- Apple cider vinegar: A popular ingredient to add tanginess to the sauce. It helps to balance the flavors out.

- Worcestershire sauce: This sauce is used to balance the flavors of the sauce perfectly.

- Brown/White sugar: Brown sugar adds a distinct flavor than white sugar, but both of them give sweet notes to the sauce. They both form great caramelization on the meat.

- Liquid sweetener: They include honey, maple syrup, corn syrup, and other sweeteners. There used to add sweet tones to the sauce and also caramelization.

- Fruits: Some fruits that can be used are dates and berries.

- Lemon juice: It adds tanginess and acidity to the sauce.

- Hot sauce: A few drops can bring up the spiciness of the BBQ sauce.

HOW TO THICKEN BBQ SAUCE?

If you are in a pinch at your grilling station and find that the sauce is too thin and is not sticking to your meat, follow the instructions below. There are other sin areas in which you want to have a thicker sauce. To thicken up your BBQ sauce quickly, you need to either:

1. In 1 cup of your barbecue sauce, add one tablespoon corn starch and one tablespoon water.

2. In 1 cup of your barbecue sauce, add two tablespoons of flour and one-fourth cup water.

To increase the viscosity of the sauce and also to enhance the flavor, you can also add splashes of heavy cream, or you can melt a few cubes of butter. This method will solve your problems.

HOW TO THIN BBQ SAUCE?

Sometimes, the sauces you buy at the store are too thick to mix well or to brush onto your meats. There is an easy way to thin those sauces. You might think that just by splashing some water, the sauce will thin out, but that will also leave your sauce dilute and less tasty. Don't add water to thin out the sauces, but try thinning ingredients instead. You just need to add a thinning agent to the sauce. Many thinning ingredients also enhance the flavor of the sauce and the meats. Examples of a few of them are listed below:

1. One tablespoon of Apple cider vinegar
2. One tablespoon of citrus juice like lemon or orange
3. One tablespoon of stock or broth of any kind
4. 1/4 cup of ketchup

HOW TO STORE BBQ SAUCE?

Making sauces beforehand is a wise decision as they can be stored easily in bulk. If you are making homemade BBQ sauces for a barbecue get together, you need to store it properly so that its flavor isn't affected by anything. You should use a quartz size mason jar to put your barbecue sauces in. Pour the sauce in the jar after it is made and tightly seal the lid. If you are making a sauce with the technique using heat such as smoking, then you should let the sauce cool down first before pouring it into the jar. Put the tightly sealed jar in the refrigerator until you need to use it.

You can use the barbecue sauces for different dishes throughout the week.

WHEN AND HOW TO BRUSH BBQ SAUCE?

When putting BBQ sauce on raw meat, you should be careful about cross-contamination. For different meats, portion out different amounts of barbecue sauce for grilling and serving the meat on the table. To ensure food safety, try putting the portions out in different color bowls. When you have brushed sauce onto meat, wash the brush thoroughly before using it for the second time.

Lots of good sauces have a sweet element to their taste. That is because sugar and other types of sweeteners are used in making that sauce. If they are exposed to heat for a long time, they can be burnt and leave a bitter taste on the meat. This is not what you want. For an optimum caramelization and no charring, brush the sauce on your chicken drum sticks, ribs or steaks at the last 10 minutes of grilling. Your meat needs to be almost cooked when you apply the sauces. It is also enough time for the sugars to produce a beautiful glaze without it burning.

HOW LONG DOES BBQ SAUCE LAST?

Homemade BBQ sauces don't last for a long time as they don't contain preservatives and additives as they have in store-bought ones. The sauces last for about a week to 10 days. Making two or three jars is enough for spreading on different dishes in this period.

Store-bought BBQ sauces can last up to 4 months after opening them and storing them in the fridge. Unopened store-bought BBQ sauces can be used till the expiration date.

HOW TO SERVE BARBECUE SAUCE?

Sauces are used in many dishes. It's almost a necessary member of the table on barbecues, but you can spread them on other meals and meats. Think beyond just drizzling and spreading sauces on raw meat. A delicious BBQ sauce can be used in multiple scenarios, and you would want to use it in everything as well. Here are some of the ways that you can use your BBQ sauces.

- **CHICKEN**: Favorite poultry of choice, prepared in many ways and eaten by many people. Lather the sauce on some baked chicken or drizzle it over chicken shreds and use it in a chicken sandwich.

- **PORK:** You can pour it on some crispy bacon or pulled pork meat to use in a sandwich.

- **BURGERS:** It's time to upgrade our burgers by using a more complex and delicious sauce then just regular old ketchup, mustard or mayonnaise. The sauce brings up the taste of the burger with every bite.

- **PIZZA:** Most people use store-bought pizza sauce to line the pizza but try using BBQ sauce instead to make a BBQ flavored pizza. Add some grilled chicken shreds or any other meat to it.

- **DIP:** You can serve this sauce alongside some French fries, nuggets, or fried chicken. Mix it with cheese and sour cream to make a sauce to dip your vegetables into.

- **TACOS AND PIES**: Mix the BBQ sauce with ground meat, sour cream and serve it as a filling of tacos and pastries. You can replace your boring potato fillings with this instead. Add it to meat-based pies or chilies.

- **FILLING:** Pair it with a meat of your choice and make a quesadilla filling. Pour it over some meat-based nachos. Flavor the beans with this sauce by dressing over them or serving beside them.

- **JUICES:** Add it to different cocktails and juices to add spiciness

- **DRESSING:** Drizzled the BBQ sauce over chicken, vegetable, or corn salads. The sauce works great as a dressing.

RECIPES INDEX

CONCLUSION

I am happy to share this cookbook with you, and I take pride in offering you an extensive array of recipes that you will love and enjoy. I hope you benefit from each of our recipes, and I am sure you will like all the recipes we have offered you. Don't hesitate to try our creative and easy-to-make recipes, and remember that I have put my heart into coming up with delicious meals for you. If you like my recipes, you can share them with acquaintances and friends. I need your encouragement to continue writing more books!
P.S. Thank you for reading this book. If you've enjoyed this book, please don't shy; drop me a line, leave feedback, or both on Amazon. I love reading feedback and your opinion is extremely important to me.

Made in the USA
Las Vegas, NV
14 December 2023

82839941R00050